AMERICAN FAMILY OF THE COLONIAL ERA

Paper Dolls in Full Color

Tom Tierney

Dover Publications, Inc., New York

Published in Canada by General Publishing Company, Ltd., 30 Lesmill Road, Don Mills, Toronto, Ontario.

Published in the United Kingdom by Constable and Company, Ltd., 10 Orange Street, London WC2H 7EG.

American Family of the Colonial Era Paper Dolls in Full Color is a new work, first published by Dover Publications, Inc., in 1983.

International Standard Book Number: 0-486-24394-X

Manufactured in the United States of America
Dover Publications, Inc., 180 Varick Street, New York, N.Y. 10014

Sarah

Ruth

Thomas

Benjamin

Plate 1

John

Prudence

Plate 2

Samuel   Hannah

Plate 3

SR

B

B

R

T

Plate 4

Plate 5

SM

H

Plate 6

Plate 7

Plate 8

Plate 9

Plate 10

Plate 11

Plate 12

Plate 13

P

J